If you long to upgrade the quality of your messages, if you want to acquire powerful presentation skills, and if you yearn to overcome your speaking fears and become a better speaker, I invite you to download a complimentary copy of my ebook, *Communicate with Confidence*, at:
http://OvercomeYourSpeakingFears.com

Empowering Business Owners to Overcome Speaking Fears Whether You're Talking with 1 Person or 1,000

Enjoy Clear and Confident Communication Skills
to Achieve Business Growth

Marjorie Saulson

THiNKaha®

An Actionable Public Speaking Journal

E-mail: info@thinkaha.com
20660 Stevens Creek Blvd., Suite 210
Cupertino, CA 95014

Published by THiNKaha®
20660 Stevens Creek Blvd., Suite 210, Cupertino, CA 95014
http://thinkaha.com
E-mail: info@thinkaha.com

First Printing: September 2019
Hardcover ISBN: 978-1-61699-305-4   1-61699-305-7
Paperback ISBN: 978-1-61699-304-7   1-61699-304-9
eBook ISBN: 978-1-61699-303-0   1-61699-303-0
Place of Publication: Silicon Valley, California, USA
Paperback Library of Congress Number: 2018914521

Trademarks

All terms mentioned in this book that are known to be trademarks or service marks have been appropriately capitalized. Neither THiNKaha, nor any of its imprints, can attest to the accuracy of this information. Use of a term in this book should not be regarded as affecting the validity of any trademark or service mark.

Warning and Disclaimer

Every effort has been made to make this book as complete and as accurate as possible. The information provided is on an "as is" basis. The author(s), publisher, and their agents assume no responsibility for errors or omissions. Nor do they assume liability or responsibility to any person or entity with respect to any loss or damages arising from the use of information contained herein.

Acknowledgements

Elizabeth Barrett Browning began her beautiful love poem to her husband, Robert Browning, with these famous words, "How do I love thee? Let me count the ways."

I honestly don't know how to count the people who have influenced the person I have become, nor the ways in which their wisdom has impacted my own understanding of life and its lessons.

So, here is a greatly abbreviated but very sincere list of those to whom I owe so much:

- ❖ My birth family—in particular, my parents, Florence and Harry Shuman of blessed memory, and my dear sister, Marsha Murav (aka the maven, Yiddish for expert)

- ❖ My husband, Saul, who is a constant source of support and encouragement; my dear children, Melinda and Eli, and Eli's beloved wife, Michele; and my dearly beloved grandchildren, who bring such joy to my life

- ❖ The many great teachers and mentors with whom it has been my privilege to study and from whom I have learned so much

- ❖ My sister and fellow students in the numerous courses I have taken and the various groups I have joined, many of whom have become dear friends

- ❖ My clients and students who show so much faith in me and from whom I learn so much in return

- ❖ My dear friends from my years of volunteer service to my synagogue, to the Women's League for Conservative Judaism, to the United Synagogue of Conservative Judaism, to the Detroit Symphony Orchestra, and to the Association of Major Symphony Orchestra Volunteers

- ❖ To all the chance-met people who have crossed my path and enhanced my life

I also wish to acknowledge and express my appreciation to Mitchell Levy for his insightful encouragement and assistance in the creation of this book, to Jenilee Maniti for her politely consistent reminders for me to get the next piece done, and to everyone in the THINKaha company who have made the creation of this book possible.

Dedication

I dedicate this book to you, and to everyone else who has the courage to bust out of the jail of their comfort zone to learn more, to become more, to build a better business, and to serve more people than you ever dreamed possible.

How to Read a THiNKaha® Book

A Note from the Publisher

The AHAthat/THiNKaha series is the CliffsNotes of the 21st century. These books are contextual in nature. Although the actual words won't change, their meaning will every time you read one as your context will change. Be ready, you will experience your own AHA moments as you read the AHA messages™ in this book. They are designed to be stand-alone actionable messages that will help you think about a project you're working on, an event, a sales deal, a personal issue, etc. differently. As you read this book, please think about the following:

1. It should only take 15–20 minutes to read this book the first time out. When you're reading, write in the underlined area one to three action items that resonate with you.

2. Mark your calendar to re-read this book again in 30 days.

3. Repeat step #1 and mark one to three more AHA messages that resonate. They will most likely be different than the first time. BTW: this is also a great time to reflect on the AHAmessages that resonated with you during your last reading.

After reading a THiNKaha book, marking your AHA messages, re-reading it, and marking more AHA messages, you'll begin to see how these books contextually apply to you. AHAthat/THiNKaha books advocate for continuous, lifelong learning. They will help you transform your AHAs into actionable items with tangible results until you no longer have to say AHA to these moments—they'll become part of your daily practice as you continue to grow and learn.

Mitchell Levy, The AHA Guy at AHAthat
publisher@thinkaha.com

THiNKaha®

Contents

Introduction

One of Henry David Thoreau's most famous quotes states, "The mass of men lead lives of quiet desperation."

I personally believe that people often feel desperate because they stay quiet.

They have an idea of something they would like to do, but don't share it because they worry about being criticized or being told that their idea is either stupid or impossible to accomplish.

They want to undertake something but hesitate to put their dream into words because words are the start of making something real. If they start to talk about it, then they may have to put themselves on the line to actually start to do it. And if they start to do it, people may reject their efforts.

Worst of all, they may simply fail to achieve their goals. Fear keeps them silent instead.

It is no surprise, then, that public speaking is generally number one on the list of what people fear the most, even ahead of the three dreaded D's of death, disease, and divorce.

How many people lose out on job opportunities and promotions that require speaking in public?

How many people fail to serve the people they are meant to serve, and fail to earn the income they desire, because they are afraid of picking up the phone and calling people?

How much time do people spend regretting the things they hadn't said that they wished they had said, or that they wish they could have said more effectively and gotten a better response?

There have been too many times in my own life when I have kept myself and my results small, either due to fear of speaking up in public or of speaking up with the wrong message or an ineffective one.

After years of my own study (continuing today), I have made it my mission to empower people in the three vital aspects of effective communication:

1) to uncover and enhance their own authentic messages
2) to acquire powerful presentation skills that engage their ideal audience
3) to overcome the nerves and fear that are keeping them silent

As a result, people can reach their highest goals and dreams by finally being free to speak up and succeed in sharing their gifts with those who have been desperately waiting for them to show up in their world and enhance their lives, to increase their income and build the business they yearn to create.

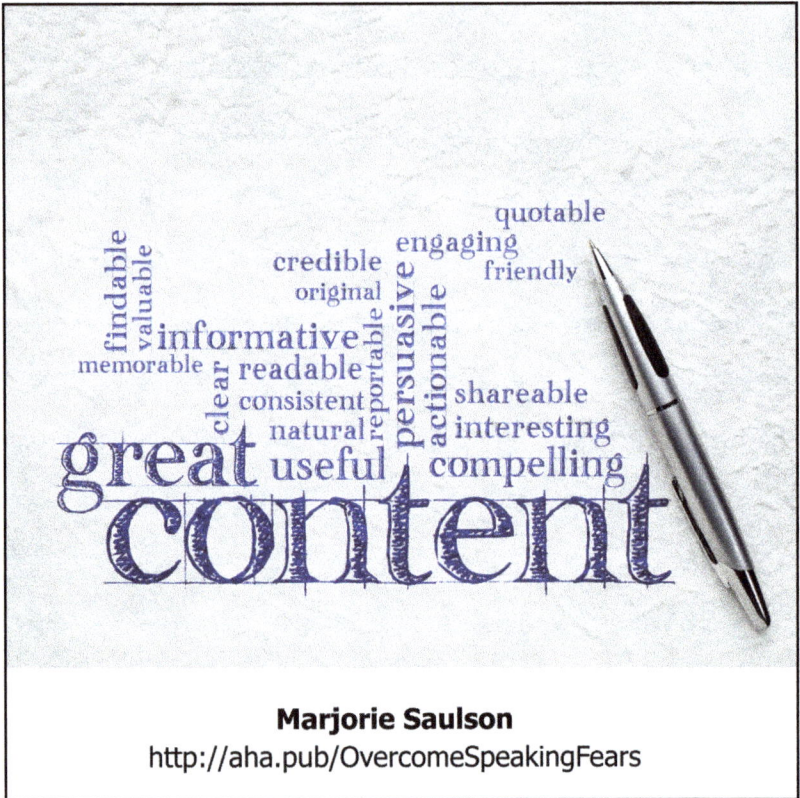

Marjorie Saulson
http://aha.pub/OvercomeSpeakingFears

Share the AHA messages from this book socially by going to
http://aha.pub/OvercomeSpeakingFears

Section I

Confident Content That Attracts Your Ideal Audience

Your well-crafted message is the foundation of speaking success. Ask yourself these questions about any message you are creating:

- ✓ Does it speak to both the pain and the desired benefits of your ideal audience?
- ✓ Are you using language that resonates with your ideal audience?
- ✓ Is your information well-organized in a proven structure that is easily followed and understood by your audience?
- ✓ Are you including one (and only one) call to action that will entice people in your audience to take the next step with you?

If you want your message to enjoy enduring value and positive results, keep in mind this warning by Thomas Bailey: "Great orators who are not also great writers become very indistinct to the generations following them."

Watch this video:
http://aha.pub/OvercomeSpeakingFearsS1

1

Public speaking occurs any time you
speak to someone other than yourself.
#ConfidentCommunicationSkills

_____

_____

_____

2

Define problems and solutions before creating a presentation. #ConfidentCommunicationSkills

_____

_____

_____

3

It is crucial for people in business to get over any speaking fears; otherwise, fear keeps you feeling small and your results small. #ConfidentCommunicationSkills

_____

_____

_____

4

To be truly successful in business, you need to feel comfortable in any speaking situation. #ConfidentCommunicationSkills

_____

_____

_____

5

An effective business person has specific marketing strategies to help deal with any sales conversations and create the best possible outcome. #ConfidentCommunicationSkills

_____

_____

_____

6

We all have areas in which we're more comfortable than others. Win over your fears to achieve the level of confidence and the results you desire. #ConfidentCommunicationSkills

_____

_____

_____

7

The fear of public speaking is just one of the many hindrances in business. It is a big one, vital to overcome. #ConfidentCommunicationSkills

_____

_____

_____

8

In today's world, most people don't talk to people. They either send emails, texts, or read things that are written. 1-on-1 communication is much more powerful. #ConfidentCommunicationSkills

_____

_____

_____

9

In public speaking, content is important. What is your message? How are you presenting it? #ConfidentCommunicationSkills

_____

_____

_____

10

Knowing your niche and what people in it "really" want is crucial to effective communication. #ConfidentCommunicationSkills

_____

_____

_____

11

Sometimes, your business conversations are affected by personal life situations that get in the way. You need to know how to handle them with grace. #ConfidentCommunicationSkills

_____

_____

_____

12

In business, understanding the language that resonates with your ideal audience is crucial to your success. Can you speak that language? #ConfidentCommunicationSkills

_____

_____

_____

13

If you want to speak effectively in public, be sure to incorporate the pain points of your audience. #ConfidentCommunicationSkills

_____

_____

_____

14

As a business person, it's important
to say something credible so that
you don't get caught flat-footed.
#ConfidentCommunicationSkills

15

To make effective #BusinessPresentations,
it's important to know the language
that will resonate with your audience.
#ConfidentCommunicationSkills

16

The combination of your confidence and willingness to be an #Influencer increases the number of people you reach and can serve. #ConfidentCommunicationSkills

_____

_____

_____

17

One way to build your confidence as a public speaker is by researching and understanding your audience. #ConfidentCommunicationSkills

_____

_____

_____

18

Keep breathing while you speak; it will improve the sound of your voice. #ConfidentCommunicationSkills

_____

_____

_____

19

Just remember that everybody's B.S. Meter is always on. Focus on being you, the real you, so those with whom you interact can know and trust you. #ConfidentCommunicationSkills

_____

_____

_____

Effective business presentations require powerful presentation skills.

Keep practicing.

#Speaker

Marjorie Saulson
http://aha.pub/OvercomeSpeakingFears

Share the AHA messages from this book socially by going to
http://aha.pub/OvercomeSpeakingFears

Section II

Prepare Like a Pro
So the Details Don't Derail You

When preparing for any presentation, phone call, or event, it pays to keep these lists in mind:

✓ **Things to <u>confirm</u> ahead of time:**
- o the date, time, and location of any meeting
- o travel time and arrangements (always allow extra time)
- o if you are speaking:
  - ▪ the length of time you are allotted to speak
  - ▪ the agenda of the event
  - ▪ the room setup (auditorium style; type of tables, if any; etc.)
  - ▪ stage? rostrum? microphone?
  - ▪ power source and screen for slides or video (if needed)
  - ▪ who will introduce you

- ✓ Things to <u>prepare</u> ahead of time for different types of events:
  - o your remarks
  - o your well-designed notes to use as needed in making your presentation
  - o any handouts you wish to give to an audience or to prospects
  - o for video or slides, all the equipment needed, plus extra backup cords
  - o your introduction (either a formal one for a speech or your informal one for networking)
  - o the main points you wish to share in any conversation
  - o clothing appropriate to the occasion
- ✓ Things to <u>bring</u> with you to any event
  - o your notes
  - o your business cards
  - o handouts (if you are using them)
  - o a copy of your introduction on a clipboard to hand to the person introducing you (who will have probably forgotten to

bring the copy of the introduction you sent ahead of time)
- o your cellphone
- o your glasses (if you wear them)
- o any other items you may need if you are making a presentation, including any hardware, software, extra cords, backup files for slide presentations, etc.

✓ **Things to do after you <u>arrive at the event</u>:**
- o Check in and let the event planner know that you have arrived.
- o Go to the restroom, both to make a comfort stop and to double check that you look as neat as you did when you left to come to the event.
- o Take care of, and double check, all technical setups if you are showing slides, etc. (Allow extra time for any glitches that may show up.)
- o Check out all the room arrangements.
- o Do a microphone check, if you will be using one.

- o Greet all the attendees personally as they arrive.
- o If it is a networking event, start out by introducing yourself to someone standing alone and looking uncomfortable.

✓ **Always remember that there are some people out there who desperately need the information that you have to share. Staying silent out of nerves or fear is cheating them out of knowledge that can enhance their lives.**

Things to do <u>after the event</u>:

- o Write a thank you note to the event organizer.
- o Make a follow-up call to request referrals for other speaking opportunities.
- o Note any changes you wish to make to improve the quality of your presentation.
- o Follow up with the people with whom it is important to connect.

Watch this video:
http://aha.pub/OvercomeSpeakingFearsS2

20

In any business discussion, it's not just about being prepared emotionally and physically. You also need to understand your ideal audience and how to create a message that truly resonates with the people in it. #ConfidentCommunicationSkills

_____

_____

_____

21

You may be smart and capable as a speaker, but if you don't always come across well, you may not have prepared well enough. #ConfidentCommunicationSkills

---

22

Effective business presentations require powerful presentation skills. Keep practicing. #Speaker #ConfidentCommunicationSkills

---

23

Well-organized notes in a large font can help reduce nervousness and ensure an effective presentation. #ConfidentCommunicationSkills

---

24

An easy way to figure out how to communicate effectively with people in your ideal audience is by interviewing them. Simply ask them about their worries and what they really want to have or achieve. #ConfidentCommunicationSkills

---

25

Your audience wants a clear and understandable definition of your services, something that they can easily resonate with and know they need. #ConfidentCommunicationSkills

_____

_____

_____

26

To find out what your target audience wants and needs, ask good questions. Listen more and talk less. Prepare for success. #ConfidentCommunicationSkills

_____

_____

_____

27

Part of being prepared for any conversation is having a list of bullet points that you can confidently share. #ConfidentCommunicationSkills

_____

_____

_____

28

Dressing appropriately includes feeling comfortable in your clothes. It affects how you present yourself in public. #ConfidentCommunicationSkills

_____

_____

_____

29

To increase your confidence, choose clothes that are appropriate for the occasion, comfortable to wear, and make you feel good in them. #ConfidentCommunicationSkills

_____

_____

_____

30

In business, even the simplest details matter, and having a system in place for all those pesky details is crucial. #ConfidentCommunicationSkills

_____

_____

_____

31

The devil is in the details. Remember that it was a faulty O-ring, a miniscule part in a huge rocket, that caused the Challenger disaster. #ConfidentCommunicationSkills

_____

_____

_____

A key sign that you have improved your #PublicSpeaking skills is when you clearly articulate a message that resonates with your audience. #ConfidentCommunicationSkills

Marjorie Saulson
http://aha.pub/OvercomeSpeakingFears

Share the AHA messages from this book socially by going to
http://aha.pub/OvercomeSpeakingFears

Section III

Rock Your Presentations

The best crafted message in the world can be absolutely ruined if its presentation is boring. Here are the three areas to consider when practicing your presentation skills for spoken messages:

1) Are you dressed both appropriately and in a way that attracts and keeps the attention of those who are looking at you?

2) Are you using movement effectively to reinforce the meaning of your remarks, or are you pacing back and forth or standing still like a statue?

3) Do you use your tone of voice, volume, pacing, and appropriate pauses to keep the eager attention of your audience on the main points you want to make?

For written messages, check out these important considerations:

1) Is your message written as a stream of consciousness in a big blob of text in a small font that the human eye cannot possibly read? (I get emails like this far too often, and I do the dance of the delete key.)

2) Is your message in a large enough font that people can easily read?

3) Is the font you are using easy to read? (Avoid script for that reason.)

4) Have you broken up the text into short paragraphs that can be read quickly by someone skimming your copy (which most people do)?

5) Have you included graphics, both for variety and to reinforce the meaning of your message?

To ensure that people will willingly, even eagerly, consume your content, make sure your presentations and messages are both interesting and easy to hear or read.

Watch this video:
http://aha.pub/OvercomeSpeakingFearsS3

32

#PublicSpeakingTips include knowing what to say — powerful messages combined with powerful presentation skills. #ConfidentCommunicationSkills

_____

_____

_____

33

Good #BusinessSkills include having polite ways to set boundaries around people who ask inappropriate questions. #ConfidentCommunicationSkills

_____

_____

_____

34

If you drop your chin to look at your notes, you lose eye contact with your audience, and your audience loses the sound of your voice. #ConfidentCommunicationSkills

_____

_____

_____

35

When you're sharing ideas, work on creating messaging that allows the listener to get your point and want to share it. #ConfidentCommunicationSkills

_____

_____

_____

36

To rock your business presentations, figure out who is in your audience and what really bothers them. #ConfidentCommunicationSkills

_____

_____

_____

37

Great communication includes clarity of speech so people can understand what you are actually saying. #ConfidentCommunicationSkills

_____

_____

_____

38

Understanding the sales process includes listening for the language that resonates with each potential client. #ConfidentCommunicationSkills

_____

_____

_____

39

You greatly increase your chances
of making a successful presentation
if you can speak in terms of your
audience's challenges and worries.
#ConfidentCommunicationSkills

_____

_____

_____

40

If you want to be successful, it is vital to be effective at reaching your audience when you are giving a presentation. #ConfidentCommunicationSkills

_____

_____

_____

41

A key sign that you have improved your #PublicSpeaking skills is when you clearly articulate a message that resonates with your audience. #ConfidentCommunicationSkills

_____

_____

_____

42

Powerful presentations are delivered in a concise, clear, understandable, and effective manner. #ConfidentCommunicationSkills

_____

_____

_____

43

When speaking publicly, it's not a good idea to read from a script. Most people sound boring when they do, so it's a recipe for disaster. #ConfidentCommunicationSkills

_____

_____

_____

44

A well-crafted and well-presented
message keeps the interest
and attention of your audience.
#ConfidentCommunicationSkills

45

Knowing exactly how you will start
and end your presentation gives
you more confidence as a speaker.
#ConfidentCommunicationSkills

46

Organized notes in a large font enable you to share your message without worrying about having to memorize it. #ConfidentCommunicationSkills

_____

_____

_____

47

Preparing well ahead of time is vital to delivering a message of value to your audience (even an audience of one). #ConfidentCommunicationSkills

---

48

Using tone variation and well-timed pauses keeps the attention of your listeners focused on you and your message. #ConfidentCommunicationSkills

---

49

Silence is a powerful indicator
that your audience is either truly
listening to you or is asleep.
#ConfidentCommunicationSkills

_____

_____

_____

50

Building excitement and interest in
your topic is vital to engaging and
keeping the attention of your audience.
#ConfidentCommunicationSkills

_____

_____

_____

51

A well-timed pause allows your listeners to appreciate the full value of what you have just said. #ConfidentCommunicationSkills

_____

_____

_____

52

Knowing and believing that you have a great message to share is a critical element of rocking your presentation. #ConfidentCommunicationSkills

_____

_____

_____

53

Speaking with one person is a conversation. Think of giving a presentation as an expanded conversation with a larger audience. #ConfidentCommunicationSkills

_____

_____

_____

54

When a speech is compelling, there is an energetic exchange between the presenter and the audience. Are you generating that energetic exchange? #ConfidentCommunicationSkills

---

55

Effective communication creates a strong emotional bond between the presenter and the audience. Are you creating that bond? #ConfidentCommunicationSkills

---

56

Humor is an incredibly powerful tool for engaging the interest and attention of your audience. Have you told any good jokes lately? #ConfidentCommunicationSkills

_____

_____

_____

57

If you share written materials with your audience, make sure the font is large enough so people can read it easily. Note: This goes for name tags as well! #ConfidentCommunicationSkills

_____

_____

_____

58

People access information in three
ways: hearing it, seeing it, and writing
it down. Are you using all three to get
your message across more effectively?
#ConfidentCommunicationSkills

_____

_____

_____

59

Most people remember very little of any speech they hear. That's the reality. That's why you need to hit the ball out of the park. #ConfidentCommunicationSkills

_____

_____

_____

60

During any business engagement, it's important to stay focused on what people are saying. #ConfidentCommunicationSkills

_____

_____

_____

61

An effective conversation between two or more people requires constant attention. Are you really listening, or are you talking AT each other? #ConfidentCommunicationSkills

_____

_____

_____

62

Whether you are speaking or singing,
your body is your instrument.
You need to keep it in tune.
#ConfidentCommunicationSkills

_____

_____

_____

63

Wear clothing that is appropriate
and in which you feel comfortable.
Otherwise, your discomfort will
show in your body language.
#ConfidentCommunicationSkills

_____

_____

_____

64

The tone of your voice will either attract or repel your listeners. A great tone of voice will increase the value of any talk. #ConfidentCommunicationSkills

_____

_____

_____

65

As a speaker, it is your responsibility to share your information clearly and concisely. Some enthusiasm doesn't hurt either. #ConfidentCommunicationSkills

_____

_____

_____

What feels like criticism might be a good suggestion in disguise. See if you can discover it. #ConfidentCommunicationSkills

Marjorie Saulson
http://aha.pub/OvercomeSpeakingFears

Share the AHA messages from this book socially by going to
http://aha.pub/OvercomeSpeakingFears

Section IV

Criticism Mindset and Heart-Set Reset to Gain the Confidence You Desire

From what I have observed, it seems as if criticism is a go-to parenting and teaching strategy to which we are often subjected on the path to becoming civilized adults.

Unfortunately, as small children, we have little ability to heal ourselves of the emotional wounds caused by that criticism. Those unhealed wounds get triggered when we are criticized in the same way we were criticized as children.

The two main strategies that I have adopted to deal with criticism may also prove helpful to you. They require purposely setting aside the pain of the criticism and coming into your adult self to ask yourself two questions:

1) Consider the source. (My husband, Saul, taught me this one.) Is the person criticizing you someone whose opinion you respect? If not, then maybe that person's criticism isn't worth respecting either.

2) Is there something here to learn? Unless you feel that you already know absolutely everything there is to know about your subject, maybe what feels like criticism is actually a good suggestion dressed up in unfortunate language.

I'd love to hear what you think of these two ideas and if you personally find them helpful. Please drop me a line at marjorie@vibrantvocalpower.com, and write "Criticism" in the subject line to share your thoughts.

Watch this video:
http://aha.pub/OvercomeSpeakingFearsS4

66

If you aren't speaking up and sharing your gifts, you are cheating the people who may desperately need them. #ConfidentCommunicationSkills

_____

_____

_____

67

Sometimes, the most difficult conversations are not in your business, but in your personal life. The same skills can apply to both. #ConfidentCommunicationSkills

_____

_____

_____

68

A vital component of communication is empathy, understanding your prospects and their pain points. #ConfidentCommunicationSkills

_____

_____

_____

69

Sales conversations are overwhelming at times. Get the right mindset and skill set to overcome your fears ahead of time. #ConfidentCommunicationSkills

---

70

What feels like criticism might be
a good suggestion in disguise.
See if you can discover it.
#ConfidentCommunicationSkills

_____

_____

_____

71

Knowing that you can handle difficult
public speaking situations can give
you a greater sense of confidence.
#ConfidentCommunicationSkills

_____

_____

_____

72

We are each responsible for our own reactions. Blaming others teaches us nothing. #ConfidentCommunicationSkills

_____

_____

_____

73

The emotional stuff can trigger old wounds from the past that were never healed. Purposely consult your adult self to handle the situation. #ConfidentCommunicationSkills

_____

_____

_____

74

People may come up with criticism that is off the wall. See if you can find something in their comments that might help you. #ConfidentCommunicationSkills

---

75

Criticism hurts. Learn to diminish its power by focusing on your value as a person. #ConfidentCommunicationSkills

---

76

Criticism can be constructive if you are open to considering new ideas that can improve what you are currently doing. #ConfidentCommunicationSkills

_____

_____

_____

77

Your job as a public speaker is to connect with the people in your ideal audience and present the benefits you can provide for them. #ConfidentCommunicationSkills

_____

_____

_____

78

There's always room for
improvement. That's one of the
things that keeps life interesting.
#ConfidentCommunicationSkills

79

The willingness to welcome
and accept change is a
sign of personal growth.
#ConfidentCommunicationSkills

We all grew up with at least some criticism, rejection, and failure. The challenge occurs when these old wounds limit our current effectiveness and happiness. #ConfidentCommunicationSkills

Marjorie Saulson
http://aha.pub/OvercomeSpeakingFears

Share the AHA messages from this book socially by going to
http://aha.pub/OvercomeSpeakingFears

Section V

Reject the Impact of Rejection So It Doesn't Affect Your Success

I don't know about you, but I learned about rejection as a kid in gym class. Since I was never the most athletically skilled person, I always seemed to get picked last for any team sport. It didn't feel very good at all.

I would stand there while the team captains were picking sides, and say inside my head, *Pick me, please pick me*, but I was never picked until there was no one else left.

Like dealing with criticism, I've had to come up with strategies to deal with the fact that there are people who say no to opportunities that I offer them.

I now view any message or offer I share as a sorting

mechanism that divides people into one or two of four categories:

1) For some people, it's a good fit at the right time.

2) For some people, it's a good fit at the wrong time.

3) For some people, it's not a good fit.

4) Some people know others for whom it might be a good fit.

Whatever the result may be, I always know that I have planted a seed of either present or future possibility.

Watch this video:
http://aha.pub/OvercomeSpeakingFearsS5

80

Your well-crafted message
is a sorting mechanism, dividing
your audience into those who are a
fit for your offer and those who aren't.
#ConfidentCommunicationSkills

_____

_____

_____

81

Instead of worrying about being asked
questions, see them as a sign of interest.
#ConfidentCommunicationSkills

_____

_____

_____

82

Showing vulnerability takes courage and is a sure sign of authenticity. #ConfidentCommunicationSkills

_____

_____

_____

83

Self-confidence comes from the belief in your own value, your ethical standards, and your integrity. #ConfidentCommunicationSkills

_____

_____

_____

84

Pain nourishes courage. You have
to fail in order to practice being brave.
—Mary Tyler Moore via Marjorie Saulson
#ConfidentCommunicationSkills

_____

_____

_____

85

We all grew up with at least some criticism,
rejection, and failure. The challenge
occurs when these old wounds limit our
current effectiveness and happiness.
#ConfidentCommunicationSkills

_____

_____

_____

86

The things that bother you on the day you're feeling tired often don't bother you when you feel rested. Get enough sleep! #ConfidentCommunicationSkills

_____

_____

_____

87

Feeling discouraged by someone shooting you down? Ask yourself this key question: Do you really respect this person's opinion? #ConfidentCommunicationSkills

_____

_____

_____

88

In dealing with rejection, can your brain find a solution that your heart cannot? #ConfidentCommunicationSkills

_____

_____

_____

89

Reject the impact of rejection by reframing your message in a way that can resonate with other people. #ConfidentCommunicationSkills

_____

_____

_____

90

Come out of your comfort zone so you can share your gift and serve the people whom you are meant to serve. #ConfidentCommunicationSkills

_____

_____

_____

91

When people say no to a well-crafted message, it either means they are not a good fit for what you offer or that this is not the right time for them to invest in it. #ConfidentCommunicationSkills

_____

_____

_____

92

Networking success is not giving out a lot of your business cards, it's getting the business cards of the right people so you can follow up with them. #ConfidentCommunicationSkills

_____

_____

_____

93

Every no is one step closer to a yes.
#ConfidentCommunicationSkills

94

It requires a certain amount
of trial and error to accomplish
business and personal growth.
#ConfidentCommunicationSkills

A temporary roadblock can become a permanent stop sign if you focus on the negative instead of the positive.
#ConfidentCommunicationSkills

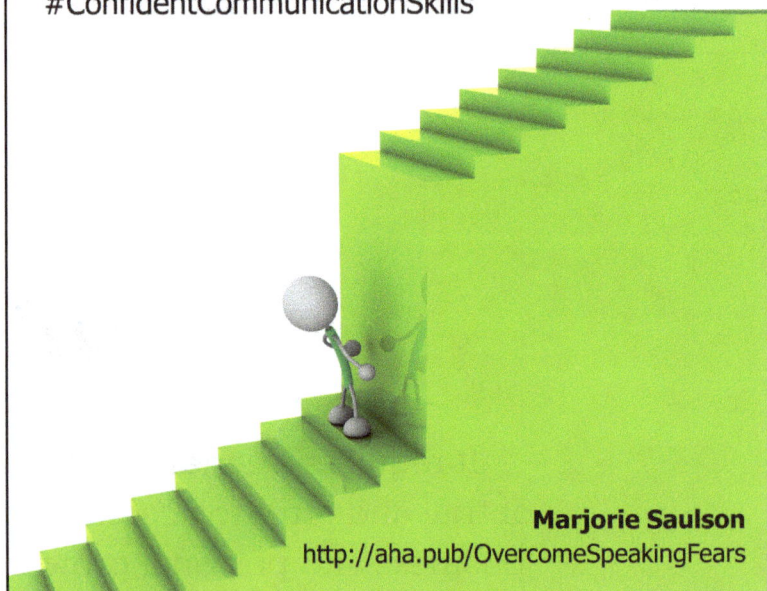

Marjorie Saulson
http://aha.pub/OvercomeSpeakingFears

Share the AHA messages from this book socially by going to
http://aha.pub/OvercomeSpeakingFears

Section VI

How to Use Failure as a Growth Strategy

One of my long-time mottos is that "nothing is a failure unless you don't learn the lesson it has to teach you."

That point is powerfully made in the title of John Maxwell's book, *Failing Forward: Turning Mistakes into Stepping Stones for Success.*

So, when something doesn't go as well as you had expected, how can you turn it around?

First, never ask yourself what went wrong. The question itself is so discouraging that it makes it difficult to get yourself going again.

Instead, ask yourself these two questions:

1) **What went right?** Take the time to acknowledge yourself (and your team, if you are working as part of a team or committee) for all that went well. Get those endorphins flowing to counteract the negative energy of something not going as well as you had hoped or expected.

2) **Where can this be improved?** You are looking at the same thing that didn't go as expected, as in the question of what went wrong, but instead of looking at it from a negative point of view, you are looking at it from a place of possibility.

When you can come from a place of possibility instead of negativity, that is when you can view something that went wrong not as a failure, but simply as a plot twist on the road to success.

Watch this video:
http://aha.pub/OvercomeSpeakingFearsS6

95

Perfection in public speaking may be admirable, but it's not relatable. It's our mistakes that often endear us to other people. #ConfidentCommunicationSkills

_____

_____

_____

96

A mistake is never a failure unless you refuse to learn the lesson it has to teach you. #ConfidentCommunicationSkills

_____

_____

_____

97

How do you use failure as a growth strategy? By learning the lesson it has to teach about what doesn't work. #ConfidentCommunicationSkills

_____

_____

_____

98

Having a system in place makes it much easier to handle speaking situations. #ConfidentCommunicationSkills

---

99

A foolish consistency is the hobgoblin of little minds. —Ralph Waldo Emerson. Think differently and try new things. #ConfidentCommunicationSkills

---

100

It's a tremendous compliment to people when you focus on them.
#ConfidentCommunicationSkills

_____

_____

_____

101

A temporary roadblock can become a permanent stop sign if you focus on the negative instead of the positive.
#ConfidentCommunicationSkills

_____

_____

_____

102

Rejection and criticism are interrelated. They both hit really hard on the emotional level. Give yourself some love to counteract them. #ConfidentCommunicationSkills

_____

_____

_____

103

A failure is only a failure if you let it stop you from working toward your end goal. #ConfidentCommunicationSkills

_____

_____

_____

104

Failure has seeds of future greatness. It's only when you're willing to fail that you can eventually succeed. #ConfidentCommunicationSkills

_____

_____

_____

105

The disease of perfectionism
is a common cause of failure.
#ConfidentCommunicationSkills

_____

_____

_____

106

When we get stuck in the standards
of perfection, it's really hard to get
out of the jail of our comfort zone.
#ConfidentCommunicationSkills

_____

_____

_____

107

The path to success is littered with failure. You can't move forward unless you are willing to do something that you're not used to doing. #ConfidentCommunicationSkills

_____

_____

_____

108

To be successful, you need to have a plan, then work your plan. #ConfidentCommunicationSkills

_____

_____

_____

109

Hugs are endorphin fixes.
#ConfidentCommunicationSkills

_____

_____

_____

110

The only way to make real progress in any
area is to be willing to do it badly at first.
You can't play center court at Wimbledon
the first time you pick up a tennis racket.
#ConfidentCommunicationSkills

_____

_____

_____

111

A road block only becomes
a failure if you refuse to learn
the lesson it has to teach.
#ConfidentCommunicationSkills

_____

_____

_____

112

When something doesn't work out the
way you had planned, acknowledge
the things that were good and worth
keeping. It encourages you to stay
on the path to eventual success.
#ConfidentCommunicationSkills

_____

_____

_____

113

View failure from a different point of view. If you don't let it stop you, it's just a plot twist. #ConfidentCommunicationSkills

_____

_____

_____

114

Ask yourself what went right instead of asking what went wrong. It's a far more encouraging way to operate. #ConfidentCommunicationSkills

_____

_____

_____

Being a little bit nervous when you're public speaking lets your audience know on a subliminal level that what you're saying is important. #ConfidentCommunicationSkills

Marjorie Saulson
http://aha.pub/OvercomeSpeakingFears

Share the AHA messages from this book socially by going to
http://aha.pub/OvercomeSpeakingFears

Section VII

Get Your Nerves to Serve You Instead of Sabotaging You

As Mark Twain famously observed, "There are two types of speakers—those who are nervous and those who are liars."

Therefore, it is absolutely natural to be nervous before you speak, especially on an important occasion. The question then becomes whether you let your nerves sink or serve you. Here are just two of the many ways they can serve you:

1) If you tend to procrastinate when getting prepared for an event, being nervous can get you to prepare your remarks sooner rather than later.

2) Let your nerves give you nervous energy so your audience picks up on that excitement, rather than being bored by a blah presentation.

For more ideas on this topic (and many others), check out my complimentary ebook, *Communicate with Confidence* at http://OvercomeYourSpeakingFears.com.

Watch this video:
http://aha.pub/OvercomeSpeakingFearsS7

115

An idea doesn't have to be your own to be worth keeping. Good ideas can come from anyone and anywhere. #ConfidentCommunicationSkills

_____

_____

_____

116

Just because we're having a problem
with something doesn't mean we have
clarity about what the problem really is.
#ConfidentCommunicationSkills

_____

_____

_____

117

The world needs to hear from you because
you have your own unique gift to share.
#ConfidentCommunicationSkills

_____

_____

_____

118

If someone asks a question you don't understand or can't answer, ask for clarity. #ConfidentCommunicationSkills

---

119

Shallow breathing and fast talking are both signs of nervousness. Avoid them in your business presentations. #ConfidentCommunicationSkills

---

120

Breathing deeply gives your body
a message that you're safe. It helps
you overcome your nervousness.
#ConfidentCommunicationSkills

_____

_____

_____

121

Not only does deep breathing as
you speak help with your nerves, it
also improves the sound of your voice.
#ConfidentCommunicationSkills

_____

_____

_____

122

Being a little bit nervous when you're public speaking lets your audience know on a subliminal level that what you're saying is important. #ConfidentCommunicationSkills

_____

_____

_____

123

Both the tone of your voice and your body language affect how the audience reacts to your message. #ConfidentCommunicationSkills

_____

_____

_____

124

Accomplishing anything of value is like doing a thousand-piece puzzle. It helps to have the overall picture in mind before you get started. #ConfidentCommunicationSkills

_____

_____

_____

125

When you're having trouble getting started on a project, begin with a couple of easy things first to get yourself going in the right direction. #ConfidentCommunicationSkills

_____

_____

_____

126

To increase your skill, knowledge, and accomplishment level, have the patience and courage to win over the fear of not doing things perfectly. #ConfidentCommunicationSkills

_____

_____

_____

127

The bigger the goal is,
the more things there are to
practice and get good at to succeed.
#ConfidentCommunicationSkills

_____

_____

_____

128

Some things you try won't go well at
first. This sometimes indicates areas
where you may need some help and
guidance to find the next right step.
#ConfidentCommunicationSkills

_____

_____

_____

129

It feels really good when you persevere and accomplish that missing piece so you can move forward. #ConfidentCommunicationSkills

_____

_____

_____

130

Sometimes when we think what we make is a mistake, it turns out to be a mistake in the right direction. #ConfidentCommunicationSkills

_____

_____

_____

131

Think of your nerves as part of your energy system. They empower you to give presentations with enthusiasm and excitement. #ConfidentCommunicationSkills

_____

_____

_____

132

There are only two types of speakers. Those who are nervous and those who are liars. —Mark Twain via Marjorie Saulson #ConfidentCommunicationSkills

_____

_____

_____

133

Even if you feel nervous, you can still come across as confident. Your audience can't see whether the butterflies in your stomach are flying in formation or not. #ConfidentCommunicationSkills

---

134

When you stay inside your comfort zone too long, it starts to feel like a jail. #ConfidentCommunicationSkills

---

When giving speeches, focus on the gifts you are offering and sharing with those who need them, instead of on your nerves.
#ConfidentCommunicationSkills

Marjorie Saulson
http://aha.pub/OvercomeSpeakingFears

Share the AHA messages from this book socially by going to
http://aha.pub/OvercomeSpeakingFears

Section VIII

Speaking with Clarity and Confidence in Any Situation

While you can plan ahead and prepare for scheduled presentations, there are many more times in life when you simply need to respond off the cuff to whatever is being discussed at the time.

Here are a few suggestions from my playbook on how to calmly and confidently answer any off-the-wall comments:

1) Clarify ahead of time the major points you wish to make should anyone ask you about your business, vacation, family, health, or whatever else may come up in a conversation.

2) Take your time. Don't let anyone stampede you into an instant answer to a comment or question.

3) Often, someone's comment or question isn't clearly stated. Ask for clarification or for an example if you're not sure how to respond.

4) If a question is about something you don't wish to discuss, simply say that you do not care to talk about that issue. (If the question is about something that is truly not that person's business, sometimes simply looking at the person with a surprised, or perhaps offended, expression is all you need to do.)

Watch this video:
http://aha.pub/OvercomeSpeakingFearsS8

135

Practice by visualizing yourself giving talks with confidence. That's just one way to handle your nerves. Basketball players visualize making baskets all the time. #ConfidentCommunicationSkills

---

136

When you don't share an important message, both you and your potential listeners lose. #ConfidentCommunicationSkills

---

137

Take a deep breath and don't take any of it too seriously. —Cher via Marjorie Saulson #ConfidentCommunicationSkills

_____

_____

_____

138

If you don't care about what you're sharing, nobody else will either. #ConfidentCommunicationSkills

_____

_____

_____

139

The better you can express yourself, the better your relationship will be with your audience. #ConfidentCommunicationSkills

_____

_____

_____

140

Sharing wisdom is one of the fundamental ways in which human beings relate to each other. Go out and speak purposely and beautifully. #ConfidentCommunicationSkills

_____

_____

_____

Marjorie's Mottos

- ➤ Nothing improves your vision like company coming.

- ➤ A professional volunteer is someone who gets aggravated for free.

- ➤ Misers make good ancestors.

- ➤ Never confuse price with value.

- ➤ Nothing beats abject terror as a motivator.

- ➤ Your opinion of me is none of my business.

- ➤ It is better to be a *has been* than a *never was*.

- ➤ If you don't schedule it, chances are, it won't get done.

- ➤ When you stay inside your comfort zone too long, it starts to feel like a jail.

- ➤ Don't let yesterday's regrets spoil the possibilities and joys of today.

- ➤ If you do not fail part of the time, you are not playing big enough.

- ➤ In life, there is no stasis. You are either shrinking or growing. Choose to grow.

Afterword

One of Abraham Lincoln's less well-known quotes is: "Give me six hours to chop down a tree, and I will spend the first four sharpening the axe."

Another version of the same thought is that we do not plan to fail, but we often fail to plan. We are so eager to jump into doing something, anything, that we don't take the time (and often lack the patience) to spend time actually thinking about what we are about to do.

Here are some questions to ask yourself before you jump off the ten-meter board into preparing your next big presentation or starting your next big job:

- ✓ What is the result, the end goal, that I want to accomplish?
- ✓ What are the various steps that are required to accomplish that end result?
- ✓ What research and resources are necessary to do a quality job?
- ✓ What specific steps are required to move the job forward?
- ✓ How much time will each step require?
- ✓ How will I schedule the necessary time for each step?
- ✓ What is the deadline to accomplish my desired result?
- ✓ When will I start?

If all these ideas and suggestions feel overwhelming, here's a final quote to keep in mind:

"The journey of a thousand miles begins with one step."
—Lao Tzu

About the Author

Business Communication Coach Marjorie Saulson is the president and CEO of Vibrant Vocal Power Inc. (https://www.vibrantvocalpower.com/).

She delights in empowering reluctant speakers, entrepreneurs, coaches, and volunteers to feel calm and confident in any speaking situation, whether they are speaking to one person or to a thousand.

Marjorie is a professionally trained singer and voice actor and often uses music and a variety of voices to get her points across in a humorous and memorable way.

She has graced the stage and led workshops in a variety of cities, including Boston, Chicago, Dallas, Detroit, Edmonton, Houston, Kansas City, Los Angeles, and Winnipeg.

THINKaha® has created AHAthat for you to share content from this book.

⊃ Share each AHA message socially:
   http://aha.pub/OvercomeSpeakingFears

⊃ Share additional content: https://AHAthat.com

⊃ Info on authoring: https://AHAthat.com/Author

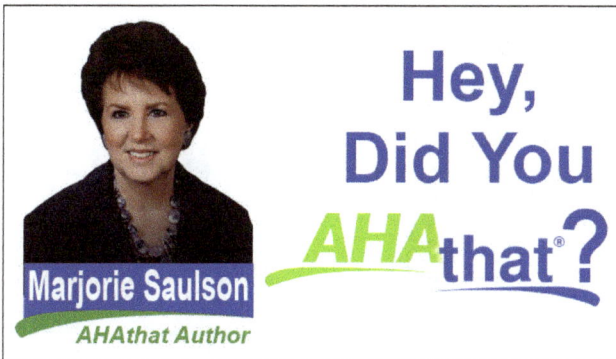

www.ingramcontent.com/pod-product-compliance
Lightning Source LLC
Chambersburg PA
CBHW060542100426
42742CB00013B/2422